I0017137

STRATEGIES FOR SOFTWARE TESTING

A FULL COMPLETE SELF-GUIDE FOR HIGH-QUALITY TESTING

ENGR. JOHN THOMAS

Copyright © 2024 ENG. JOHN THOMAS

All rights reserved. No part of this publlcation may be reproduced, distributed or transmitted in any form or by any means including photocopying, recording, or other electronic or mechanical methods, without the prior written permission of the publisher

Contents

Software Testing 6

   Why to Learn Software Testing? 6

   Applications of Software Testing 7

Software Testing - Overview 10

Software Testing - Myths 16

Software Testing - QA, QC & Testing 21

   Testing, Quality Assurance,and Quality Control 21

   Audit and Inspection 23

   Testing and Debugging 24

Software Testing - ISO Standards 26

   ISO/IEC 9126 26

   ISO/IEC 9241-11 27

   ISO/IEC 25000:2005 28

   ISO/IEC 12119 29

   Miscellaneous 29

Software Testing - Types of Testing 32

   Manual Testing 32

   Automation Testing 32

What to Automate?.. 33

When to Automate?... 34

How to Automate? 34

Software Testing Tools 35

Software Testing - Methods.. 37

Black-Box Testing 37

White-Box Testing 39

Grey-Box Testing 41

A Comparison of Testing Methods............................... 43

Software Testing - Levels 46

Functional Testing 46

Unit Testing 48

Integration Testing 49

System Testing 50

Regression Testing 51

Acceptance Testing 52

Alpha Testing... 53

Beta Testing... 54

Non-Functional Testing 55

Usability Testing 58

Security Testing 59

Portability Testing 60

Software Testing - Documentation 62

Test Plan 62

Test Scenario 63

Test Case 64

Traceability Matrix 65

Software Testing - Estimation Techniques 67

Functional Point Analysis 67

Test Point Analysis... 67

Mark-II Method 68

Miscellaneous... 68

CONCLUSION... 69

Software Testing

Testing is the process of evaluating a system or its component(s) with the intent to find whether it satisfies the specified requirements or not.

Testing is executing a system in order to identify any gaps, errors, or missing requirements in contrary to the actual requirements.

This book will give you a basic understanding on software testing, its types, methods, levels, and other related terminologies.

Why to Learn Software Testing?

In the IT industry, large companies have a team with responsibilities to evaluate the developed software in context of the given requirements. Moreover, developers also conduct testing which is called **Unit Testing**. In most cases, the following professionals are involved in testing a system within their respective capacities –

- Software Tester
- Software Developer

- Project Lead/Manager
- End User

Different companies have different designations for people who test the software on the basis of their experience and knowledge such as Software Tester, Software Quality Assurance Engineer, QA Analyst, etc.

Applications of Software Testing

- **Cost Effective Development** - Early testing saves both time and cost in many aspects, however reducing the cost without testing may result in improper design of a software application rendering the product useless.
- **Product Improvement** - During the SDLC phases, testing is never a time-consuming process. However diagnosing and fixing the errors identified during proper testing is a time-consuming but productive activity.
- **Test Automation** - Test Automation reduces the testing time, but it is not possible to start test automation at any time during software development. Test automaton should be started when the software has been manually tested and is

stable to some extent. Moreover, test automation can never be used if requirements keep changing.

- **Quality Check** - Software testing helps in determining following set of properties of any software such as
  - o Functionality
  - o Reliability
  - o Usability
  - o Efficiency
  - o Maintainability
  - o Portability

This book is designed for software testing professionals who would like to understand the Testing Framework in detail along with its types, methods, and levels. This book provides enough ingredients to start with the software testing process from where you can take yourself to higher levels of expertise.

Before proceeding with this book, you should have a basic understanding of the software development life cycle (SDLC). In addition, you should have a basic understanding of software programming using any programming language.

Software Testing - Overview

What is Testing?

Testing is the process of evaluating a system or its component(s) with the intent to find whether it satisfies the specified requirements or not. In simple words, testing is executing a system in order to identify any gaps, errors, or missing requirements in contrary to the actual requirements.

According to ANSI/IEEE 1059 standard, Testing can be defined as - A process of analyzing a software item to detect the differences between existing and required conditions (that is defects/errors/bugs) and to evaluate the features of the software item.

Who does Testing?

It depends on the process and the associated stakeholders of the project(s). In the IT industry, large companies have a team with responsibilities to evaluate the developed software in context of the given requirements. Moreover, developers also conduct testing which is called **Unit Testing**. In most cases, the following professionals are involved in testing a system within their respective capacities –

- Software Tester
- Software Developer
- Project Lead/Manager
- End User

Different companies have different designations for people who test the software on the basis of their experience and knowledge such as Software Tester, Software Quality Assurance Engineer, QA Analyst, etc.

It is not possible to test the software at any time during its cycle. The next two sections state when testing should be started and when to end it during the SDLC.

When to Start Testing?

An early start to testing reduces the cost and time to rework and produce error-free software that is delivered to the client. However in Software Development Life Cycle (SDLC), testing can be started from the Requirements

Gathering phase and continued till the deployment of the software.

It also depends on the development model that is being used. For example, in the Waterfall model, formal testing is conducted in the testing phase; but in the incremental model, testing is performed at the end of every increment/iteration and the whole application is tested at the end.

Testing is done in different forms at every phase of SDLC –

- During the requirement gathering phase, the analysis and verification of requirements are also considered as testing.
- Reviewing the design in the design phase with the intent to improve the design is also considered as testing.
- Testing performed by a developer on completion of the code is also categorized as testing.

When to Stop Testing?

It is difficult to determine when to stop testing, as testing is a never-ending process and no one can claim that a software is 100% tested. The following aspects are to be considered for stopping the testing process –

- Testing Deadlines
- Completion of test case execution
- Completion of functional and code coverage to a certain point
- Bug rate falls below a certain level and no high-priority bugs are identified
- Management decision

Verification & Validation

These two terms are very confusing for most people, who use them interchangeably. The following table highlights the differences between verification and validation.

Sr.No.	Verification	Validation
1	Verification addresses the concern: "Are you building it you building it	Validation addresses the concern: "Are you building the right thing?"

	right?"	
2	Ensures that the software system meets all the functionality.	Ensures that the functionalities meet the intended behavior.
3	Verification takes place first and includes the checking for documentation, code, etc.	Validation occurs after verification and mainly involves the checking of the overall product.
4	Done by developers.	Done by testers.
5	It has static activities, as it includes collecting reviews,	It has dynamic activities, as it includes executing the software against the requirements.

walkthroughs, and inspections to verify a software.

It is an objective process and no subjective decision should be needed to verify a software.

6

It is a subjective process and involves subjective decisions on how well a software works.

Software Testing - Myths

Given below are some of the most common myths about software testing.

Myth 1: Testing is Too Expensive

Reality – There is a saying, pay less for testing during software development or pay more for maintenance or correction later. Early testing saves both time and cost in many aspects, however reducing the cost without testing may result in improper design of a software application rendering the product useless.

Myth 2: Testing is Time-Consuming

Reality – During the SDLC phases, testing is never a time-consuming process. However diagnosing and fixing the errors identified during proper testing is a time-consuming but productive activity.

Myth 3: Only Fully Developed Products are Tested

Reality – No doubt, testing depends on the source code but reviewing requirements and developing test cases is independent from the developed code. However iterative or incremental approach as a development life cycle model may reduce the dependency of testing on the fully developed software.

Myth 4: Complete Testing is Possible

Reality – It becomes an issue when a client or tester thinks that complete testing is possible. It is possible that all paths have been tested by the team but occurrence of complete testing is never possible. There might be some scenarios that are never executed by the test team or the client during the software development life cycle and may be executed once the project has been deployed.

Myth 5: A Tested Software is Bug-Free

Reality – This is a very common myth that the clients, project managers, and the management team believes in. No one can claim with absolute certainty that a software application is 100% bug-free even if a tester with superb testing skills has tested the application.

Myth 6: Missed Defects are due to Testers

Reality – It is not a correct approach to blame testers for bugs that remain in the application even after testing has been performed. This myth relates to Time, Cost, and Requirements changing Constraints. However the test strategy may also result in bugs being missed by the testing team.

Myth 7: Testers are Responsible for Quality of Product

Reality – It is a very common misinterpretation that only testers or the testing team should be responsible for product quality. Testers' responsibilities include the identification of bugs to the stakeholders and then it is their decision whether they will fix the bug or release the software. Releasing the software at the time puts more pressure on the testers, as they will be blamed for any error.

Myth 8: Test Automation should be used wherever possible to Reduce Time

Reality – Yes, it is true that Test Automation reduces the testing time, but it is not possible to start test automation at any time during software development. Test automaton should be started when the software has been manually tested and is stable to some extent. Moreover, test automation can never be used if requirements keep changing.

Myth 9: Anyone can Test a Software Application

Reality – People outside the IT industry think and even believe that anyone can test a software and testing is not a creative job. However testers know very well that this is a myth. Thinking alternative scenarios, try to crash a software with the intent to explore potential bugs is not possible for the person who developed it.

Myth 10: A Tester's only Task is to Find Bugs

Reality – Finding bugs in a software is the task of the testers, but at the same time, they are domain experts of the particular software. Developers are only responsible for the specific component or area that is assigned to them but testers understand the overall workings of the software, what the dependencies are, and the impacts of one module on another module.

—

Software Testing - QA, QC & Testing

Testing, Quality Assurance,and Quality Control

Most people get confused when it comes to pin down the differences among Quality Assurance, Quality Control, and Testing. Although they are interrelated and to some extent, they can be considered as same activities, but there exist distinguishing points that set them apart. The following table lists the points that differentiate QA, QC, and Testing.

Quality Assurance	Quality Control	Testing
QA includes activities that ensure the implementation of processes, procedures and standards in	It includes activities that ensure the verification of a developed software with respect to	It includes activities that ensure the identification of bugs/error/defects in a software.

context to verification of developed software and intended requirements.	documented (or not in some cases) requirements.	
Focuses on processes and procedures rather than conducting actual testing on the system.	Focuses on actual testing by executing the software with an aim to identify bug/defect through implementation of procedures and process.	Focuses on actual testing.
Process-oriented activities.	Product-oriented activities.	Product-oriented activities.

| Preventive activities. | It is a corrective process. | It is a preventive process. |
| It is a subset of Software Test Life Cycle (STLC). | QC can be considered as the subset of Quality Assurance. | Testing is the subset of Quality Control. |

Audit and Inspection

Audit – It is a systematic process to determine how the actual testing process is conducted within an organization or a team. Generally, it is an independent examination of processes involved during the testing of a software. As per IEEE, it is a review of documented processes that organizations implement and follow. Types of audit include Legal Compliance Audit, Internal Audit, and System Audit.

Inspection – It is a formal technique that involves formal or informal technical reviews of any artifact by identifying any error or gap. As per IEEE94, inspection is a formal evaluation technique in which software requirements, designs, or codes are examined in detail by a person or a group other than the author to detect faults, violations of development standards, and other problems.

Formal inspection meetings may include the following processes: Planning, Overview Preparation, Inspection Meeting, Rework, and Follow-up.

Testing and Debugging

Testing – It involves identifying bug/error/defect in a software without correcting it. Normally professionals with a quality assurance background are involved in bugs identification. Testing is performed in the testing phase.

Debugging – It involves identifying, isolating, and fixing the problems/bugs. Developers who code the software conduct debugging upon encountering an error in the code. Debugging is a part of White Box Testing or Unit Testing. Debugging can be performed in the development phase while conducting Unit Testing or in phases while fixing the reported bugs.

Software Testing - ISO Standards

Many organizations around the globe develop and implement different standards to improve the quality needs of their software. This chapter briefly describes some of the widely used standards related to Quality Assurance and Testing.

ISO/IEC 9126

This standard deals with the following aspects to determine the quality of a software application –

- Quality model
- External metrics
- Internal metrics
- Quality in use metrics

This standard presents some set of quality attributes for any software such as –

- Functionality
- Reliability
- Usability

- Efficiency
- Maintainability
- Portability

The above-mentioned quality attributes are further divided into sub-factors, which you can study when you study the standard in detail.

ISO/IEC 9241-11

Part 11 of this standard deals with the extent to which a product can be used by specified users to achieve specified goals with Effectiveness, Efficiency and Satisfaction in a specified context of use.

This standard proposed a framework that describes the usability components and the relationship between them. In this standard, the usability is considered in terms of user performance and satisfaction. According to ISO 9241-11, usability depends on context of use and the level of usability will change as the context changes.

ISO/IEC 25000:2005

ISO/IEC 25000:2005 is commonly known as the standard that provides the guidelines for Software Quality Requirements and Evaluation (SQuaRE). This standard helps in organizing and enhancing the process related to software quality requirements and their evaluations. In reality, ISO-25000 replaces the two old ISO standards, i.e. ISO-9126 and ISO-14598.

SQuaRE is divided into sub-parts such as –

- ISO 2500n – Quality Management Division
- ISO 2501n – Quality Model Division
- ISO 2502n – Quality Measurement Division
- ISO 2503n – Quality Requirements Division
- ISO 2504n – Quality Evaluation Division

The main contents of SQuaRE are –

- Terms and definitions
- Reference Models
- General guide
- Individual division guides

- Standard related to Requirement Engineering (i.e. specification, planning, measurement and evaluation process)

ISO/IEC 12119

This standard deals with software packages delivered to the client. It does not focus or deal with the clients' production process. The main contents are related to the following items –

- Set of requirements for software packages.
- Instructions for testing a delivered software package against the specified requirements.

Miscellaneous

Some of the other standards related to QA and Testing processes are mentioned below –

Sr.No	Standard & Description
1	**IEEE 829** A standard for the format of documents used in different stages of software testing.

IEEE 1061

2

A methodology for establishing quality requirements, identifying, implementing, analyzing, and validating the process, and product of software quality metrics.

3

IEEE 1059

Guide for Software Verification and Validation Plans.

4

IEEE 1008

A standard for unit testing.

5

IEEE 1012

A standard for Software Verification and Validation.

6

IEEE 1028

A standard for software inspections.

7

IEEE 1044

A standard for the classification of software anomalies.

8

IEEE 1044-1

A guide for the classification of software anomalies.

9

IEEE 830

A   guide   for   developing   system   requirements

specifications.

10   IEEE 730

A standard for software quality assurance plans.

11   IEEE 1061

A standard for software quality metrics and methodology.

12   IEEE 12207

A standard for software life cycle processes and life cycle data.

13   BS 7925-1

A vocabulary of terms used in software testing.

14   BS 7925-2

A standard for software component testing.

Software Testing - Types of Testing

This section describes the different types of testing that may be used to test a software during SDLC.

Manual Testing

Manual testing includes testing a software manually, i.e., without using any automated tool or any script. In this type, the tester takes over the role of an end-user and tests the software to identify any unexpected behavior or bug. There are different stages for manual testing such as unit testing, integration testing, system testing, and user acceptance testing.

Testers use test plans, test cases, or test scenarios to test a software to ensure the completeness of testing. Manual testing also includes exploratory testing, as testers explore the software to identify errors in it.

Automation Testing

Automation testing, which is also known as Test Automation, is when the tester writes scripts and uses another software to test the product. This process involves automation of a manual process. Automation Testing is used to re-run the test scenarios that were performed manually, quickly, and repeatedly.

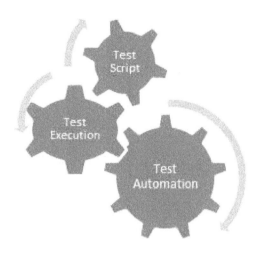

Apart from regression testing, automation testing is also used to test the application from load, performance, and stress point of view. It increases the test coverage, improves accuracy, and saves time and money in comparison to manual testing.

What to Automate?

It is not possible to automate everything in a software. The areas at which a user can make transactions such as the login form or registration forms, any area where large number of users can access the software simultaneously should be automated.

Furthermore, all GUI items, connections with databases, field validations, etc. can be efficiently tested by automating the manual process.

When to Automate?

Test Automation should be used by considering the following aspects of a software −

- Large and critical projects
- Projects that require testing the same areas frequently
- Requirements not changing frequently
- Accessing the application for load and performance with many virtual users
- Stable software with respect to manual testing
- Availability of time

How to Automate?

Automation is done by using a supportive computer language like VB scripting and an automated software application. There are many tools available that can be used to write automation scripts. Before mentioning the tools, let us identify the process that can be used to automate the testing process –

- Identifying areas within a software for automation
- Selection of appropriate tool for test automation
- Writing test scripts
- Development of test suits
- Execution of scripts
- Create result reports
- Identify any potential bug or performance issues

Software Testing Tools

The following tools can be used for automation testing –

- HP Quick Test Professional
- Selenium
- IBM Rational Functional Tester
- SilkTest
- TestComplete
- Testing Anywhere
- WinRunner
- LoadRunner

- Visual Studio Test Professional
- WATIR

Software Testing - Methods

There are different methods that can be used for software testing. This chapter briefly describes the methods available.

Black-Box Testing

The technique of testing without having any knowledge of the interior workings of the application is called black-box testing. The tester is oblivious to the system architecture and does not have access to the source code. Typically, while performing a black-box test, a tester will interact with the system's user interface by providing inputs and examining outputs without knowing how and where the inputs are worked upon.

The following table lists the advantages and disadvantages of black-box testing.

Advantages	Disadvantages
Well suited and efficient for large	Limited coverage, since only a selected number of test scenarios is actually

code segments.	performed.
Code access is not required.	Inefficient testing, due to the fact that the tester only has limited knowledge about an application.
Clearly separates user's perspective from the developer's perspective through visibly defined roles.	Blind coverage, since the tester cannot target specific code segments or errorprone areas.
Large numbers of moderately skilled testers can test the application with no knowledge of implementation, programming language, or	The test cases are difficult to design.

operating systems.

White-Box Testing

White-box testing is the detailed investigation of internal logic and structure of the code. White-box testing is also called **glass testing** or **open-box testing**. In order to perform **white-box** testing on an application, a tester needs to know the internal workings of the code.

The tester needs to have a look inside the source code and find out which unit/chunk of the code is behaving inappropriately.

The following table lists the advantages and disadvantages of white-box testing.

Advantages	Disadvantages
As the tester has knowledge of the source code, it becomes very easy to find out which type of data can help in testing the application effectively.	Due to the fact that a skilled tester is needed to perform

It helps in optimizing the code.

Extra lines of code can be removed which can bring in hidden defects.

white-box testing, the costs are increased.

Sometimes it is impossible to look into every nook and corner to find out hidden errors that may create problems, as many paths will go untested.

It is difficult to maintain white-box testing, as it requires specialized

tools like code
analyzers and
debugging
tools.

Due to the tester's knowledge about the code, maximum coverage is attained during test scenario writing.

Grey-Box Testing

Grey-box testing is a technique to test the application with having a limited knowledge of the internal workings of an application. In software testing, the phrase the more you know, the better carries a lot of weight while testing an application.

Mastering the domain of a system always gives the tester an edge over someone with limited domain knowledge. Unlike black-box testing, where the tester only tests the application's user interface; in grey-box testing, the tester has access to design documents and the database. Having this knowledge, a tester can prepare better test data and test scenarios while making a test plan.

Advantages	Disadvantages
Offers combined benefits of black-box and white-box testing wherever possible.	Since the access to source code is not available, the ability to go over the code and test coverage is limited.
Grey box testers don't rely on the source code; instead they rely on interface definition and functional specifications.	The tests can be redundant if the software designer has already run a test case.
Based on the limited information available, a grey-box tester can design excellent test	Testing every possible input stream is unrealistic because it would take an unreasonable amount of time; therefore, many program paths will

scenarios especially   go untested.
around
communication
protocols and data
type handling.

The test is done from
the point of view of
the user and not the
designer.

A Comparison of Testing Methods

The following table lists the points that differentiate black-box testing, grey-box testing, and white-box testing.

Black-Box Testing	Grey-Box Testing	White-Box Testing
The internal workings of an application need not be known.	The tester has limited knowledge of the internal workings of the	Tester has full knowledge of the internal workings of the application.

		application.
Also known as closed-box testing, data-driven testing, or functional testing.	Also known as translucent testing, as the tester has limited knowledge of the insides of the application.	Also known as clear-box testing, structural testing, or code-based testing.
Performed by end-users and also by testers and developers.	Performed by end-users and also by testers and developers.	Normally done by testers and developers.
Testing is based on external expectations - Internal behavior of the application is unknown.	Testing is done on the basis of high-level database diagrams and data flow diagrams.	Internal workings are fully known and the tester can design test data accordingly.

It is exhaustive and the least time-consuming.	Partly time-consuming and exhaustive.	The most exhaustive and time-consuming type of testing.
Not suited for algorithm testing.	Not suited for algorithm testing.	Suited for algorithm testing.
This can only be done by trial-and-error method.	Data domains and internal boundaries can be tested, if known.	Data domains and internal boundaries can be better tested.

Software Testing - Levels

There are different levels during the process of testing. In this chapter, a brief description is provided about these levels.

Levels of testing include different methodologies that can be used while conducting software testing. The main levels of software testing are –

- Functional Testing
- Non-functional Testing

Functional Testing

This is a type of black-box testing that is based on the specifications of the software that is to be tested. The application is tested by providing input and then the results are examined that need to conform to the functionality it was intended for. Functional testing of a software is conducted on a complete, integrated system to evaluate the system's compliance with its specified requirements.

There are five steps that are involved while testing an application for functionality.

Steps **Description**

Steps	Description
I	The determination of the functionality that the intended application is meant to perform.
II	The creation of test data based on the specifications of the application.
III	The output based on the test data and the specifications of the application.
IV	The writing of test scenarios and the execution of test cases.
V	The comparison of actual and expected results based on the executed test cases.

An effective testing practice will see the above steps applied to the testing policies of every organization and hence it will make sure that the organization maintains the strictest of standards when it comes to software quality.

Unit Testing

This type of testing is performed by developers before the setup is handed over to the testing team to formally execute the test cases. Unit testing is performed by the respective developers on the individual units of source code assigned areas. The developers use test data that is different from the test data of the quality assurance team.

The goal of unit testing is to isolate each part of the program and show that individual parts are correct in terms of requirements and functionality.

Limitations of Unit Testing

Testing cannot catch each and every bug in an application. It is impossible to evaluate every execution path in every software application. The same is the case with unit testing.

There is a limit to the number of scenarios and test data that a developer can use to verify a source code. After having exhausted all the options, there is no choice but to stop unit testing and merge the code segment with other units.

Integration Testing

Integration testing is defined as the testing of combined parts of an application to determine if they function correctly. Integration testing can be done in two ways: Bottom-up integration testing and Top-down integration testing.

Sr.No.	Integration Testing Method
1	**Bottom-up integration** This testing begins with unit testing, followed by tests of progressively higher-level combinations of units called modules or builds.
2	**Top-down integration** In this testing, the highest-level modules are tested first and progressively, lower-level modules are tested thereafter.

In a comprehensive software development environment, bottom-up testing is usually done first, followed by top-down testing. The process concludes with multiple tests of the complete application, preferably in scenarios designed to mimic actual situations.

System Testing

System testing tests the system as a whole. Once all the components are integrated, the application as a whole is tested rigorously to see that it meets the specified Quality Standards. This type of testing is performed by a specialized testing team.

System testing is important because of the following reasons −

- System testing is the first step in the Software Development Life Cycle, where the application is tested as a whole.
- The application is tested thoroughly to verify that it meets the functional and technical specifications.

- The application is tested in an environment that is very close to the production environment where the application will be deployed.
- System testing enables us to test, verify, and validate both the business requirements as well as the application architecture.

Regression Testing

Whenever a change in a software application is made, it is quite possible that other areas within the application have been affected by this change. Regression testing is performed to verify that a fixed bug hasn't resulted in another functionality or business rule violation. The intent of regression testing is to ensure that a change, such as a bug fix should not result in another fault being uncovered in the application.

Regression testing is important because of the following reasons −

- Minimize the gaps in testing when an application with changes made has to be tested.

- Testing the new changes to verify that the changes made did not affect any other area of the application.
- Mitigates risks when regression testing is performed on the application.
- Test coverage is increased without compromising timelines.
- Increase speed to market the product.

Acceptance Testing

This is arguably the most important type of testing, as it is conducted by the Quality Assurance Team who will gauge whether the application meets the intended specifications and satisfies the client's requirement. The QA team will have a set of pre-written scenarios and test cases that will be used to test the application.

More ideas will be shared about the application and more tests can be performed on it to gauge its accuracy and the reasons why the project was initiated. Acceptance tests are not only intended to point out simple spelling mistakes, cosmetic errors, or interface gaps, but also to point out any bugs in the application that will result in system crashes or major errors in the application.

By performing acceptance tests on an application, the testing team will reduce how the application will perform in production. There are also legal and contractual requirements for acceptance of the system.

Alpha Testing

This test is the first stage of testing and will be performed amongst the teams (developer and QA teams). Unit testing, integration testing and system testing when combined together is known as alpha testing. During this phase, the following aspects will be tested in the application –

- Spelling Mistakes
- Broken Links
- Cloudy Directions
- The Application will be tested on machines with the lowest specification to test loading times and any latency problems.

Beta Testing

This test is performed after alpha testing has been successfully performed. In beta testing, a sample of the intended audience tests the application. Beta testing is also known as **pre-release testing**. Beta test versions of software are ideally distributed to a wide audience on the Web, partly to give the program a "real-world" test and partly to provide a preview of the next release. In this phase, the audience will be testing the following –

- Users will install, run the application and send their feedback to the project team.
- Typographical errors, confusing application flow, and even crashes.
- Getting the feedback, the project team can fix the problems before releasing the software to the actual users.
- The more issues you fix that solve real user problems, the higher the quality of your application will be.
- Having a higher-quality application when release it to the general public will increase customer satisfaction.

Non-Functional Testing

This section is based upon testing an application from its non-functional attributes. Non-functional testing involves testing a software from the requirements which are nonfunctional in nature but important such as performance, security, user interface, etc.

Some of the important and commonly used non-functional testing types are discussed below.

Performance Testing

It is mostly used to identify any bottlenecks or performance issues rather than finding bugs in a software. There are different causes that contribute in lowering the performance of a software –

- Network delay
- Client-side processing
- Database transaction processing
- Load balancing between servers
- Data rendering

Performance testing is considered as one of the important and mandatory testing type in terms of the following aspects –

- Speed (i.e. Response Time, data rendering and accessing)
- Capacity
- Stability
- Scalability

Performance testing can be either qualitative or quantitative and can be divided into different sub-types such as **Load testing** and **Stress testing**.

Load Testing

It is a process of testing the behavior of a software by applying maximum load in terms of software accessing and manipulating large input data. It can be done at both normal and peak load conditions. This type of testing identifies the maximum capacity of software and its behavior at peak time.

Most of the time, load testing is performed with the help of automated tools such as Load Runner, AppLoader, IBM

Rational Performance Tester, Apache JMeter, Silk Performer, Visual Studio Load Test, etc.

Virtual users (VUsers) are defined in the automated testing tool and the script is executed to verify the load testing for the software. The number of users can be increased or decreased concurrently or incrementally based upon the requirements.

Stress Testing

Stress testing includes testing the behavior of a software under abnormal conditions. For example, it may include taking away some resources or applying a load beyond the actual load limit.

The aim of stress testing is to test the software by applying the load to the system and taking over the resources used by the software to identify the breaking point. This testing can be performed by testing different scenarios such as −

- Shutdown or restart of network ports randomly
- Turning the database on or off
- Running different processes that consume resources such as CPU, memory, server, etc.

Usability Testing

Usability testing is a black-box technique and is used to identify any error(s) and improvements in the software by observing the users through their usage and operation.

According to Nielsen, usability can be defined in terms of five factors, i.e. efficiency of use, learn-ability, memory-ability, errors/safety, and satisfaction. According to him, the usability of a product will be good and the system is usable if it possesses the above factors.

Nigel Bevan and Macleod considered that usability is the quality requirement that can be measured as the outcome of interactions with a computer system. This requirement can be fulfilled and the end-user will be satisfied if the intended goals are achieved effectively with the use of proper resources.

Molich in 2000 stated that a user-friendly system should fulfill the following five goals, i.e., easy to Learn, easy to remember, efficient to use, satisfactory to use, and easy to understand.

In addition to the different definitions of usability, there are some standards and quality models and methods that define usability in the form of attributes and sub-attributes such as ISO-9126, ISO-9241-11, ISO-13407, and IEEE std.610.12, etc.

UI vs Usability Testing

UI testing involves testing the Graphical User Interface of the Software. UI testing ensures that the GUI functions according to the requirements and tested in terms of color, alignment, size, and other properties.

On the other hand, usability testing ensures a good and user-friendly GUI that can be easily handled. UI testing can be considered as a sub-part of usability testing.

Security Testing

Security testing involves testing a software in order to identify any flaws and gaps from security and vulnerability point of view. Listed below are the main aspects that security testing should ensure –

- Confidentiality

- Integrity
- Authentication
- Availability
- Authorization
- Non-repudiation
- Software is secure against known and unknown vulnerabilities
- Software data is secure
- Software is according to all security regulations
- Input checking and validation
- SQL insertion attacks
- Injection flaws
- Session management issues
- Cross-site scripting attacks
- Buffer overflows vulnerabilities
- Directory traversal attacks

Portability Testing

Portability testing includes testing a software with the aim to ensure its reusability and that it can be moved from another software as well. Following are the strategies that can be used for portability testing –

- Transferring an installed software from one computer to another.
- Building executable (.exe) to run the software on different platforms.

Portability testing can be considered as one of the sub-parts of system testing, as this testing type includes overall testing of a software with respect to its usage over different environments. Computer hardware, operating systems, and browsers are the major focus of portability testing. Some of the pre-conditions for portability testing are as follows –

- Software should be designed and coded, keeping in mind the portability requirements.
- Unit testing has been performed on the associated components.
- Integration testing has been performed.
- Test environment has been established.

Software Testing - Documentation

Testing documentation involves the documentation of artifacts that should be developed before or during the testing of Software.

Documentation for software testing helps in estimating the testing effort required, test coverage, requirement tracking/tracing, etc. This section describes some of the commonly used documented artifacts related to software testing such as –

- Test Plan
- Test Scenario
- Test Case
- Traceability Matrix

Test Plan

A test plan outlines the strategy that will be used to test an application, the resources that will be used, the test environment in which testing will be performed, and the limitations of the testing and the schedule of testing activities. Typically the Quality Assurance Team Lead will be responsible for writing a Test Plan.

A test plan includes the following –

- Introduction to the Test Plan document
- Assumptions while testing the application
- List of test cases included in testing the application
- List of features to be tested
- What sort of approach to use while testing the software
- List of deliverables that need to be tested
- The resources allocated for testing the application
- Any risks involved during the testing process
- A schedule of tasks and milestones to be achieved

Test Scenario

It is a one line statement that notifies what area in the application will be tested. Test scenarios are used to ensure that all process flows are tested from end to end. A particular area of an application can have as little as one test scenario to a few hundred scenarios depending on the magnitude and complexity of the application.

The terms 'test scenario' and 'test cases' are used interchangeably, however a test scenario has several steps, whereas a test case has a single step. Viewed from this perspective, test scenarios are test cases, but they include several test cases and the sequence that they should be executed. Apart from this, each test is dependent on the output from the previous test.

Test Case

Test cases involve a set of steps, conditions, and inputs that can be used while performing testing tasks. The main intent of this activity is to ensure whether a software passes or fails in terms of its functionality and other aspects. There are many types of test cases such as functional, negative, error, logical test cases, physical test cases, UI test cases, etc.

Furthermore, test cases are written to keep track of the testing coverage of a software. Generally, there are no formal templates that can be used during test case writing. However, the following components are always available and included in every test case –

- Test case ID

- Product module

- Product version

- Revision history

- Purpose

- Assumptions

- Pre-conditions

- Steps

- Expected outcome

- Actual outcome

- Post-conditions

Many test cases can be derived from a single test scenario. In addition, sometimes multiple test cases are written for a single software which are collectively known as test suites.

Traceability Matrix

Traceability Matrix (also known as Requirement Traceability Matrix - RTM) is a table that is used to trace the requirements during the Software Development Life Cycle. It can be used for forward tracing (i.e. from Requirements to Design or Coding) or backward (i.e. from

Coding to Requirements). There are many user-defined templates for RTM.

Each requirement in the RTM document is linked with its associated test case so that testing can be done as per the mentioned requirements. Furthermore, Bug ID is also included and linked with its associated requirements and test case. The main goals for this matrix are –

- Make sure the software is developed as per the mentioned requirements.
- Helps in finding the root cause of any bug.
- Helps in tracing the developed documents during different phases of SDLC.

Software Testing - Estimation Techniques

Estimating the efforts required for testing is one of the major and important tasks in SDLC. Correct estimation helps in testing the software with maximum coverage. This section describes some of the techniques that can be useful in estimating the efforts required for testing.

Functional Point Analysis

This method is based on the analysis of functional user requirements of the software with the following categories –

- Outputs
- Inquiries
- Inputs
- Internal files
- External files

Test Point Analysis

This estimation process is used for function point analysis for black-box or acceptance testing. The main elements of this method are: Size, Productivity, Strategy, Interfacing, Complexity, and Uniformity.

Mark-II Method

It is an estimation method used for analyzing and measuring the estimation based on end-user's functional view. The procedure for Mark-II method is as follows –

- Determine the viewpoint
- Purpose and type of count
- Define the boundary of count
- Identify the logical transactions
- Identify and categorize data entity types
- Count the input data element types
- Count the functional size

Miscellaneous

You can use other popular estimation techniques such as –

- Delphi Technique
- Analogy Based Estimation
- Test Case Enumeration Based Estimation
- Task (Activity) based Estimation
- IFPUG method

CONCLUSION

In the conclusion of "Software Testing," we are reminded of the indispensable role that testing plays in the development and deployment of software. Through meticulous examination and evaluation, software testers ensure that the final product meets the highest standards of quality, reliability, and functionality. However, this book also underscores the evolving nature of software testing, emphasizing the need for continuous learning and adaptation to keep pace with the ever-changing landscape of technology.

As we reflect on the insights gleaned from these pages, it becomes clear that effective software testing is not merely a technical task but a mindset—a commitment to precision, thoroughness, and innovation. From manual testing methodologies to automated testing frameworks, each approach offers unique advantages and challenges, yet all contribute to the overarching goal of delivering superior software products to end-users.

Moreover, "Software Testing" highlights the importance of collaboration and communication within interdisciplinary teams. By fostering open dialogue and mutual respect among developers, testers, and stakeholders, organizations can cultivate a culture of quality assurance that permeates every stage of the software development lifecycle.

As we bid farewell to these pages, let us carry forward the lessons learned and the principles espoused within. Let us embrace the spirit of inquiry, the pursuit of excellence, and the resilience to confront challenges head-on. For in the dynamic realm of software development, testing is not just a phase—it is a journey, one that requires dedication, diligence, and a relentless pursuit of perfection.

www.ingramcontent.com/pod-product-compliance
Lightning Source LLC
LaVergne TN
LVHW051749050326
832903LV00029B/2803